Cacophonic Contemplations

Romita Munshi

BookLeaf
Publishing

India | USA | UK

Presentation by *BookLeaf Publishing*

Web: www.bookleafpub.com

E-mail: info@bookleafpub.com

ISBN: 9789360943271

First edition 2024

PREFACE

This book has been in the making for many years and written at different points in my life. It is a reflection of my ruminations at that point in my life and my thoughts around different life events. I hope while reading through the different poems you can feel my thoughts come to life and learn a little bit about me.

Writing these poems has been cathartic for me to deal with the different stages and events in my life. If there are people experiencing similar emotions, I hope that the book gives them comfort that they are not alone.

Remembering You

I remember you everyday, since the last day
But today was different, you feel farther away
It was like a punch in my gut, a weird sensation
This knot in my stomach, some deep-rooted tension

I see your face, as the wallpaper on my phone
But can't smell you, hug you or feel your tone
Although my life continues to go on, charging ahead
Sometimes, my life feels empty, unhappy, full of dread

And some days, like today, out of the blue, I get that hit
And this grief so acute, on my being is completely writ
But, what am I going to do about it, other than with it deal
Isn't life just grief with moments of happiness you steal?

I try to keep myself distracted, find more moments of glee
Running from one distraction to another to not feel agony
But today, The Room feels extra desolate without you
And so, today, I will allow myself to be sad and be blue

Motherhood

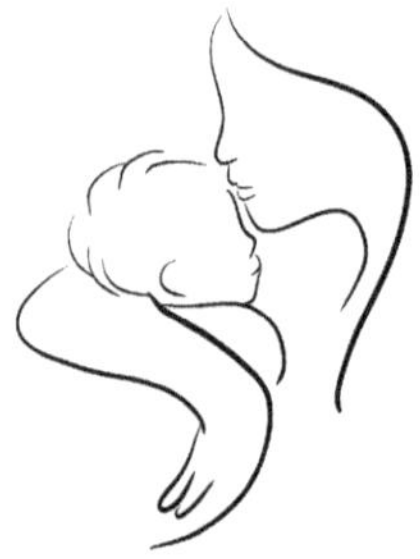

In a cocoon, lay the spawn enveloped
With love, affection, care in the reams roped
Fear in the heart who held her
Concern for the tiny font of vigour
Concern for the small wisp of hair on her head
The smile might fade away, a dread
Apprehension for her future
Fear of the slightest base tincture
And the constant strive for what's good
That's what encompasses motherhood

Maman

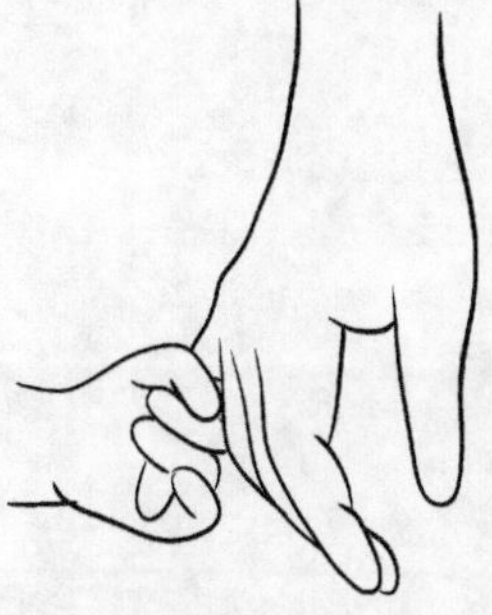

It's been six years since I last saw you
Since I last held you and gave you a hug
The void and the wound still feel brand new
A sound here, a smell there, at my heartstrings tug

It feels surreal, you not being here next to me
It feels like a punch in the gut every time I realise
That that day, was the last time together for us to be
The pain, the agony, the frustration, I cannot surmise

You taught me everything I know today
You made the woman I have proudly become
And yet, with me, you had such a brief, short stay
Even with people around, it feels sometimes lonesome

It feels like only yesterday, not so long ago
That you and I were together, hugging and laughing
And yet it feels aeons have passed us so
That all I do now is look at photos, through them rummaging

I miss you Mamma, I miss you everyday
There are times when I cry and times when I smile
I miss you when I am doing things or idling time away
I hold you in my heart, despite distance of many a mile

I love you Mamma, I'll love you everyday till the end
I love you with all my soul and heart
To my broken heart, your smiling photo does tend
I hold you close to me, even though so far apart

A wish, A prayer

I wished I could be her shield
I prayed her troubles go away
I wished I could take all her pain
And keep all the ills far at bay

I wished I could make her strong
To fight this fight for her
I prayed a lot to make it right
Set things to as it were

She cared for me all her life
Protected me, come what might
Then it was my turn to keep her safe
Defeat the demons with a fight

I thought my duty was to fight long and hard
Fight away, because born that away
Quitters we weren't, never were
It was encrypted in our DNA

It was a long battle, very hard
Hoped prayers would let us sail ahead
As everyday dawned after every night
We tried to carry on in a good stead

I wished, I prayed, I prayed, I wished
I prayed and wished everyday
But, sadly we lost the fight
And I lost my happy beam of ray

My mother's daughter

Who am I, I sometimes wonder
Away from her, asunder
Who am I, with many a thought
Sometimes amounting to naught

Who am I, this woman of nearly thirty-five
Sometimes angry, sometimes on a happy high
Sometimes full of passion
Always trying to have compassion

To be soft but still be strong
As life continues to flow along
Over time I realise that after all
I am my mother's daughter is all I recall

The journey of a lone tear

The traveler, forlorn and desolate
Traversing the glistening skin
The soft boulevard, his path had no akin

His inception, at the kohl-rimmed gate
From those very eyes which grasped and pled
As things slipped away, they bled

The vista, surreal and azure
As he made his way, trying to halt, in vain
Not realising the best choice was to be a drop in the rain

He tried hard, but was thorny to resist the lure
Of freedom from the daggers of pain and melancholy
To be able to run free, without an iota of misery

The silence reverberating, the cacophony tacit
As if the whole humanity waiting, anticipating
On the supple skin, he left his engraving

The tear reached his end, and with the drift
Plunged into the echelons of the unknown
As he lost his identity in the rain, still alone

The Night

I stand on the terrace, silent and cold
I see the building, dominating and bold
I feel the wind, not stopping for me
Flowing without barriers, flowing so free

I see the sealink, decked up with light
I see the cars on it, look like without might
I feel the wind across my face, like the passing car
Which feels it as it travels near and far

I dare not look down, from so high up here
I dare to look far away to calm my fear
I dare to look at the chimney spewing fire
Located amidst the dark and thick concrete mire

I go back inside as if my mother calls out my name
Away from contemplation and fear which can maim
And as I sit away from freedom, safe from height
I crave the contemplative cacophony of the night

Tempest

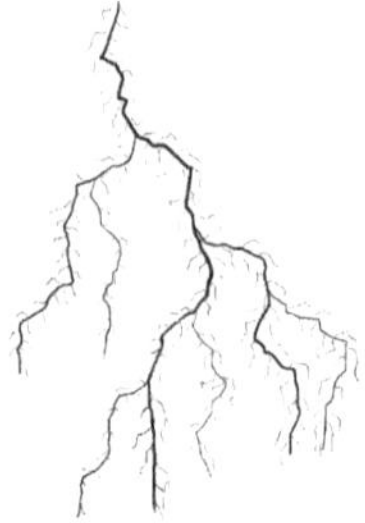

The rain, sinister and callous, surged
The clouds, laden and ominous, poured
The beads, chaste and sheer, fell
From the night firmament towards hell
They cleansed the terrain, the foliage
As if washing away the transgressions and rage
From the arena of contemporary mankind
To ameliorate our digression from the redundant grind
The divinity, showing its wrath
At the narcissistic verve, the soul sought
The thunder, vociferous and antagonistic
The lightning, assailing and frenetic
Striking the hapless milieu
A providence which was not due
The riotous shower showered ceaselessly
As it changed its tenor to benign and kindly
It then, caressed the earth with an ardour
That was bereft of its bygone gleam of fervour
And as the storm reckoned to a tranquil
I drifted into another world by my window sill

Happiness

On Mondays, when the day feels a lot
I wonder to myself and think a little thought
What is happiness, can it be caught?
Can it be learnt? Can it be taught?

On Tuesdays and Wednesdays, I tumble along
I paint a small painting, I sing a little song
I learn a bit of Korean, get a lot of words wrong
I lift some weights and try to get strong

When Thursdays and Fridays arrive, the sky feels blue
I feel like I have a bunch of things to do
I see the weekend close and it feels so true
Maybe there are things that are happy and things to rue

And as Saturday and Sunday roll by
I look back at the week with a cup of chai
Maybe this is my happiness that I imply
Maybe happiness isn't so far, but quite nearby

And Life Goes On

The water continues to ebb and flow
The sun continues to rise and set low
Into a million pieces the heart can be torn
But inevitably, life does continue to go on

Decisions can be bad, they can be wrong
Choices that make days tiresome, long
But out of those choices, decisions; life is born
And despite them, life continues to go on

You can be at the top of the world, happy and bright
When all at once, nothing seems to be right
In the hands of the world's forces, you are just a pawn
So, what can you do? Other than make life go on

You see someone die, you see a birth
From the outer space, you see a tiny earth
When all is done and all is gone
The universe continues and life goes on

The many lives we live

A life to live
A life to stay
A life to take it all away
A life to walk
Past the unknown
A life to go
Beyond the moon

A life to grieve
A life to die
A life to wake up and cry
A life to feel
The pain in the world
A life to lie
On the couch, alone and curled

A life to forgive
A life to know
A life to let it all go
A life to forget it all
And live without pain
A life to forgive grudges
And sit back and enjoy the rain

A life to enjoy life
A life to be what you want
Without giving a thought to "can't"
A life to see it all
And feel the world within your palm
A life to live life
And sit back and enjoy the calm

The silent walk

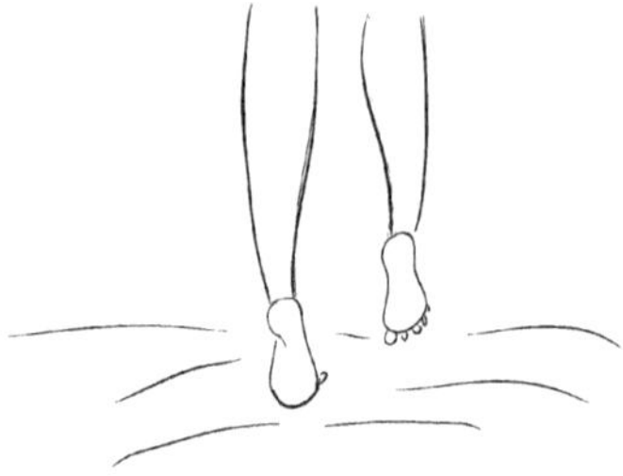

I walked all alone, in the dark, desolate corridor
Enjoying the omnipotent silence, as if by a moor
Every gasp, every partake of breath, I hear, with every step I take
A lurking danger, something unknown, I fear, with each move I make
The pristine moonlight filtering through the windows
Make the corridors seem like a destined walk to the gallows
The stillness seemed to stifle all noise in the territory
The only thing heard, was calm, a sense of eerie
By fear or fatigue or both, I made my way to my room
And tried to sleep, as the darkness continued to loom

Sojourn at the Bridge

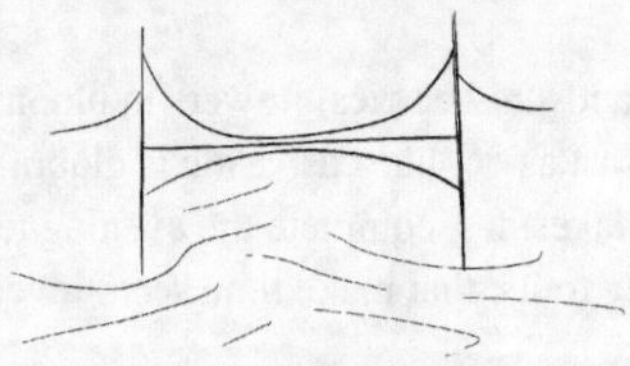

As I stood on the bridge, watching the brook pass under
To the sheer splendour of the panorama, I did surrender
The ducks, russet, noir and blanche, added vivacity to the scene
The flowers, exquisite, pied and vivid, enhanced the sheen
The sky, azure and jovial, conveyed the exultant state
The clouds, white and buoyant, opened the bliss' floodgate
The mountains, soaring over the vale, trying to reach the sky
As I yearned, fiercely and fervently, that I could go that high
The peaks, snowcapped and cold, sent out a warm impression
That even brought the gloomy out of their bouts of depression
The water, pristine and sapphire, flowing as if without a concern
The air, chaste and revitalizing, rejuvenated all without a discern
The vista, emerald and tranquil, eased my aesthetic senses
The opportunity, not to be missed, erased all grievances
And as I wafted to the enclosed space, away from this freedom
I wished I didn't have to ever return to a mundane life of boredom

Wishes

Blueberries and strawberries, flowers in bloom
Aspersions cast aside, like cast aside is gloom
Sunsets and lakesides, complete the evening tea
Facets adding traits, that make time seem lovely

Mountains and clouds, looming all around and over
Little wood cottages, providing shelter and cover
Lakes transpiring from the azure firmament
As if the two were in holy matrimony meant

Trains chugging across the emerald fields
People enjoying what the earth lovingly yields
As the sun sets to let the child of night take duty
The earth welcomes it without a trace of ennui

As the stark white moon begins its short day
The lush fields with the wispy breeze sway
Like the infant put to peaceful sleep by its mother
The caresses put flora and fauna into a slumber

The waters calm, serene as the tranquil cobalt
A place where a flash of brilliance comes to halt
To light up the dark streets and lonely lives
As the sun into oblivion and beyond dives

As the day changes from dusk to night
The birds go forth with their returning rite
And as the old sun gives way to the new moon
I wish this world would dawn very soon

Living life

A life is born
Like the fruit from its flower
Life thrives
Till it has to surrender

Life is smooth
Like the touch of a morning breeze
Life is tough
Surviving obstacles is a prestige

Life gives a chance
To experience wonders around us
The things we take for granted
Such things simple as a bee buzz

Life in itself
Is a gift to be treasured
Yet we expect
More treasures to be discovered

Life is to be enjoyed
Not just lived
Life is to be appreciated
Not just grieved

Life is a journey
That starts in a womb
Traverses through many a path
And finally ends in a tomb

Existence can be dull
But life? Never
Existence can end
The memories continue forever

Enjoy every moment
Because the same will not again knock
Stop! And notice!
Forget the ticking clock

Enjoy the laughter
Enjoy the tears
Enjoy the celebrations
Enjoy the fears

Because you might
Not be able to enjoy
One day, the same emotions
Till the next blue moon sky

Life is to be re-lived
Not survived
Life is to be remembered
Not decried

The Zephyr

A whiff, a kiss, the zephyr went on its eternal quest
Through my hair, hurtling, its pace diminish lest
Past my ear, murmuring dulcet nothings
The breeze around me enveloping
Pallid in colour, vivid in vigour
She brought fiery, tempest fervour
The plethora of mortals, towering or diminutive
Danced fanatically as if intuitive
And as I surrendered to life's pernicious ire
The passion didn't seem so dire

The grief of today

Place a hand on the pulse of the living civilization
You will feel trauma, melancholy and trepidation
Listen to the world's tacit, yet strident heartbeat
You will hear screams, mute and wilted in the heat
The heat of pain, of despair, of entities that deride you
The heat, proscribing you of all that you want and is due
Take a look around; see the shards of reason fall through
As the world plummets into the gorge of irk and rue
As the world gives in to the demands of fight and fights
As the planet is depriving itself of the plethora of basic rights
As souls, visceral and spiritual, are losing faith and hope
As dreams, great and trivial, have lost their goal and scope
As the world is trying to take steps to "make it a better place"
Can you not help but sense that it is falling from grace?

Lockdown thoughts in
May '20

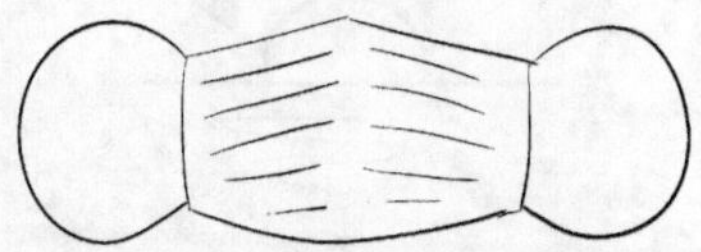

It's been two months, but who is keeping track
Life's been weird, different, somewhat out of whack
Looking at the empty street, stuck inside my home
Is this the new normal? Within these four walls I roam?

The food seems tastier, I enjoy it a whole lot more
The gym feels far away, I miss that early morning roar
The routine is in shambles, a lot more Netflix involved
Is this the new normal? Till the vaccine problem is solved?

The traffic is gone, yet the work hours seem longer
There is no switch now to disconnect, recharge, get stronger
Minutes spill into hours, spill into days, without a blink
Is this the new normal? When next, for cheers, will glasses clink?

I reminisce about my travels, seem a lifetime ago
I dream about countries to visit, cities to go
I think about when travel will again occur
Is this the new normal? Where days seem a blur?

I read about the migrant labourers, uncertain and scared
I read about those diagnosed, wonder what's going on in their head
I think about the job losses and salary cuts, the pressure they feel
Is this the new normal? Real life being stranger than reel?

I tell myself I should be so lucky to be able to do this
To lock down, to have food and water, to not have anything amiss
I ask myself, will the world be different when it opens again
Is this the new normal? A new reality we should all entertain?

Thoughts at sunset

I stood in the sand, by the sea that murmured
As if telling me secrets that got me enamoured
The orange shadows, lighting up the horizon
Something so tangible, yet an abstraction

I felt myself calm down, felt so serene
Didn't feel like an endless productivity machine
I could just stand still and enjoy that moment
Cacophony of waves, yet peaceful and silent

I was miles and hours away from home
Yet felt at home as I looked at the foam
What is it about the vast endless sea
That makes people feel so high, so free

And as the sun started to go down
Into the seas, it dived to drown
With that, the night sky grew around me
And I felt so content and not so empty

My Little Trip

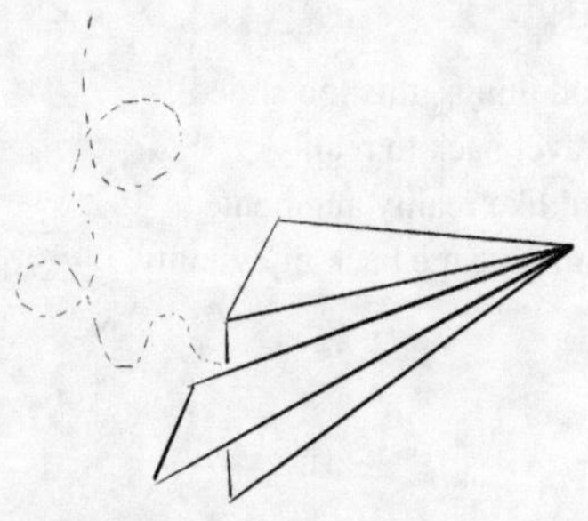

I travelled a small trip
After what seemed ages
I ventured to take a dip
In the world's many pages

I never realised till then
How much travel meant to me
Travel for a month, a day or ten
Is all it takes for me to feel free

I travelled alone, but wasn't lonely
I saw many sights, big and small
Still felt like there was more to see
How I wish I could capture it all

I met new people and old friends
I did things exciting and mundane
I tried out Instagram reels and trends
To keep all these in the memory lane

I felt the cold fall breeze in my face
The sparkling city lights enticed me
By the seashore, saw the waves race
Making me dance and filling me with glee

But like all good things, this too ended
And I had to travel back to reality
The trip seemed like reality augmented
And managed to give me back my vitality

Peace at the beach

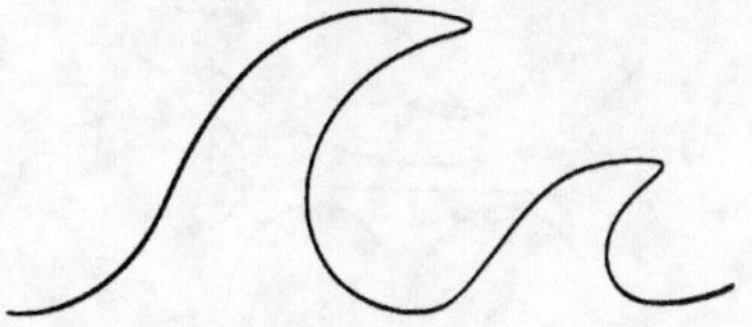

I'm at the beach, so vast across
The waves, they seem to crash and toss
I stand and stare at the void so blue
A sense of peace looking at the calm hue

The sun up high, so bright and hot
The cool breeze, reducing heat to naught
I look around, people far and few
This feeling so old, yet so new

I cannot always put into many a word
The feelings within me that are always stirred
Sometimes excitement, sometimes calm
But always, always such a balm

A balm from the rush, fast-paced life
A relief from the pressures and strife
And at that moment by the wave
I finally have the peace I crave

Boundless and Infinite

I watch the low clouds hovering
Enveloping the solid sea link
Across the water, over the land blurring
Boundless and Infinite, over the brink

I see the little people down below
Covered in colored umbrellas galore
You see all kinds of people come and go
Happy and glum, enthused and sore

Seeing the white infinity put forth you
Covering the sea link for the infinite view
Wonder about restrictions that hold you
Barriers to prevent finding new avenue

The happy free and the glum bound
Based on choices made, thrust upon
For the sore, those decisions hound
The enthused, through decisions reborn

To be happy, to be enthused, to be free
Go after what the heart seeks to be
Boundless, beyond what you hear and see
Infinite dreams, above and beyond infinity

Doom scrolling

What is this device, is it my friend?
Lying in bed, swiping on till no end
Attached to my hand, stuck to my finger
On anything, my sparse attention does not linger

Watching people argue on Twitter, sorry X
Next up is Instagram, where people flex
Facebook is maybe once in a very rare blue moon
YouTube shorts are the latest to watch people croon

Without a thought liking, mindlessly scrolling
Buncha tryhards continuously trolling
What is the world devolving to, I often wonder
Society coming apart at its seams, asunder

And yet, when I am caught in a situation I hate
I turn to this device to escape my fate
It is a quick escape, a low-effort reset
A dopamine hit through the cats I can't pet

The Onsen dip

There are very few things that can be life-changing
One of them is an Onsen dip on a winter morning
The emotions are varied, exhilarating and unchallenging
Emotions that are freeing and so so liberating

Nestled in the mountains, so serene, so quiet
A stream of sunlight, flowing through, flooding
Illuminating the entire atmosphere, so so bright
All relaxed, all worries in my life gone, absconding

As I sink into the warm mellow hug from the pool
I wonder if this is what humans were always meant to do
To connect with nature and live without a rule
Instead of sitting at desks and being all blue

The art of cultivating hobbies

We all have that bit of personal creative
That bit that wants to be innovative
But often, the fear to start them stalls us
And then we end up missing that bus

The way, I see it, it's not that tough
A way to actually get out of life's slough
A way to let loose, take a break, relax
A way to feel better from life's setbacks

Only starting something new is hard
Let the vision in, drop your guard
Embrace and feel your inner thoughts
That should help resolve all the mental knots

Hobbies come in all shapes and sizes
Each one within contains all these prizes
Pure pleasure and personal playtime
Can be even as simple as making a rhyme

People collect stamps, build matchstick castles
Some design sweaters or intricate tassels
Some like to master the art of origami
Some may pick up the arduous task of taxonomy

Whatever tickles your fancy, go for it
Set aside time and space, only a bit
It doesn't take much time in a day
Have a good time, make some hay

Cultivate and express that artist within
Take your personal creativity out for a spin
This is basically your own personal joyride
Some time to connect with yourself, set aside

So go out and find something that interests you
Instead of sitting around and being blue
Something to make your day despite other event
A way to be happy, fulfilled and content

Young and Foolish

To be young and foolish
To have such passion
To feel emotions so strong
Without any ration
To let them run amok
And show no restraint
To let it all flow
And not be faint
Sometimes it was anger
Sometimes acute sorrow
Everything I felt
In it I wallow
For it was all-consuming
Around and abound
The fervour enveloping
Leaving me astound
Then it slowly pulled away
Pulling at the strings
I tried to hold on
But felt the stings
When it all settled down
Ceasing to exist
I felt so empty
Like a hollow mist
When all was gone
Forever and long
I questioned myself
Should my emotions be so strong?
But that is the beauty
Of being so young
The option to be foolish
And recover even when stung

The Joy of Nostalgia

Sitting at my desk, writing down these lines
With nostalgia the heart beats and pines
The older I get the more nostalgic I become
Memories better defined, not so much of a scrum

I play the happy ones on constant repeat
The sad ones from the side do constantly greet
This bittersweet longing to belong in the past
Melancholia, on my mood and mind, cast

I think of sitting by the terrace, watching the sea
Chatting with my mother, drinking a cup of tea
The evening orange sun setting down so low
Sounds of happiness, time of laughter, around us glow

It is with peace and delight, I recall that time
A time truly joyous, must be in its prime
I remember the warmth I felt around me
It does fill me with sadness, but also with glee

Nostalgia, is a funny thing I believe
Making us happy but also making us grieve
The yearning for the past in which I wallow
To enjoy the warmth from the past, which I borrow

Maybe I am a masochist, to dwell in nostalgia
To enjoy it and fester the emotional myalgia
But don't you agree there is joy in reminiscing
To visit the past and enjoy what you are missing

The meditative practice of art

A flick of a hand, a smooth transient stroke
The artist within me stirring, moving, awoke
I see my vision coming alive, stirring to life
Conflicting thoughts in my mind no longer at strife

My focus remains on the movement of the brush
The canvas my playground, different ideas flush
In that moment, it is only me, the paints and the canvas
What I want to paint, through my inner dialogue I canvass

The calmness comes through as I start my work
Some remnant thoughts in the background do lurk
But as I get more engrossed with the stroke of paint
All my worry and anxiety grows more and more faint

With this ardent focus, is easy to tune out the noise
Bereft of any thought, I feel light like a genoise
And for those few moments, I stay in my peaceful cocoon
As I work on my painting and sing a little tune

The women in my life

Sometimes I ponder to myself out loud
If I can be so lucky, to be so proud
To be surrounded by women so amazing
Who do things brave and downright brazen

Some of them, firecrackers of joy
Lighting up rooms and moods, oh boy
Some have the courage to follow a road
Different from what social norms bode

Some of them reach far into the sky
Charging ahead, not an iota of shy
Some of them save lives day and night
Strong, shining beacons of hope and light

I'm around strong women who care for a soul
A human, or a fur baby, creatures big and small
I know women who work hard at what they do
Women who with integrity, go after what they pursue

I am grateful to know women who travel far
Regale me with their stories, unique or bizarre
I am fortunate to know them and each unique story
To live in their times and see them in their glory

I truly am thankful to be surrounded by them all
Who have had an impact on me, big or small
And last but not least, I'm most thankful to my mother
Without whom, I wouldn't appreciate any other

Poetry, for me

I first fell in love with poetry
A form of speech, so interlocutory
When Wordsworth wrote about daffodils
As I read his words, the time stills

And then I learnt about Ogden Nash
In such a short body, humor can stash
And I found poetry that made me smile
Poetic devices that bemuse and beguile

Then I discovered poems of W.B Yeats
Such beauty contained within those beats
And how the poems can be so individual
Stringing up a complete whole audiovisual

And so I thought, that maybe I should too
Write a bit of poetry, make some miscue
Maybe someone will enjoy my wordplay
Maybe it brings a smile or brightens their day

www.ingramcontent.com/pod-product-compliance
Lightning Source LLC
Chambersburg PA
CBHW061729130726
47996CB00006B/2571